SMALL
BEGINNINGS

SMALL BEGINNINGS

THINGS PEOPLE SAY
ABOUT BABIES

Compiled by

Nanette Newman

A GRAHAM TARRANT BOOK

David & Charles

Newton Abbot · London · North Pomfret (Vt)

For Mary Malcolm
with love

British Library Cataloguing in Publication Data

Small beginnings:things people say about
babies.
1. Parent and child—Literary collections
I. Newman, Nanette
809′ .933520431   PN6071.P29/

ISBN 0-7153-8868-1

Printed in Hong Kong

for David & Charles Publishers plc
Brunel House Newton Abbot Devon

Designed by Vic Giolitto
Typeset by P&M Typesetting Ltd., Exeter

CONTENTS

FOREWORD

I HAVE TWO DAUGHTERS and I fell in love with them immediately they were born, and happily it's a love affair that has gone on and on. It's had its patchy moments, of course, (what love affair doesn't?) but the joys and tribulations have made me realise that – although science may present us with earth-shattering discoveries, and mankind may reach for pinnacles of knowledge while at the same time inventing means of destroying life – the act of conceiving, developing and producing a baby will always be the single most wondrous human happening, and the emotion that lifts it above all others is love.

As you look at this new, crumpled being, your common sense may tell you that babies similar to your own are being born all over the world, but your heart tells you that yours is special – a one-off and quite unique.

Motherhood is universal and men and women in the past, and no doubt in the future, will write about it; some eulogistically, some cynically and some with humour and tenderness.

For this book I have chosen a cross-section to be enjoyed, I hope, by those who have had babies or by those approaching parenthood, who think as I do that reading what people feel about bringing a new life into the world is worth remembering.

NANETTE NEWMAN

INFANT JOY

'I have no name:
'I am but two days old.'
What shall I call thee?
'I happy am,
'Joy is my name.'
Sweet joy befall thee!

Pretty joy!
Sweet joy but two days old,
Sweet joy I call thee:
Thou dost smile,
I sing the while,
Sweet joy befall thee!

WILLIAM BLAKE

[8]

LITTLE EXPECTATIONS

I HAD EXPECTED SO LITTLE, really. I never expect much. I had been told of the ugliness of newborn children, of their red and wrinkled faces, their waxy covering, their emaciated limbs, their hairy cheeks, their piercing cries. All I can say is that mine was beautiful and in my defence I must add that others said she was beautiful too. She was not red nor even wrinkled, but palely soft, each feature delicately reposed in its right place, and she was not bald but adorned with a thick, startling crop of black hair ... And her eyes that seemed to see me and that looked into mine with deep gravity and charm, were a profound blue, the whites white with the gleam of alarming health. When they asked if they could have her back and put her back in her cradle for the night, I handed her over without reluctance, for the delight of holding her was too much for me. I felt as well as they that such pleasure should be regulated and rationed.

MARGARET DRABBLE from *The Millstone*

Baby Talk

As dr johnson was riding in a carriage through London on a rainy day, he overtook a poor woman carrying a baby, without any protection from the weather. Making the driver stop the coach, he invited the poor woman to get in with the child, which she did. After she had seated herself, the Doctor said to her: 'My good woman, I think it most likely that the motion of the coach will wake your child in a little while, and I wish you to understand that if you talk any baby-talk to it, you will have to get out of the coach.' As the Doctor had anticipated, the child soon awoke, and the forgetful mother exclaimed to it: 'Oh! the little dear, is he going to open his *eyesy-pysy?*' 'Stop the coach, driver!' shouted Johnson; and the woman had to get out, and finish her journey on foot.

JOHN TIMBS

LULLABY

Sleep, baby, sleep:
Sweet baby, go to sleep.
Too sweet for words, how could you tell
How sweet my baby is –
More than the trees on every hill,
More than every blade of grass,
More than all the stars in the sky,
More than the rice stalks in the field?
This babe asleep
Is more, more sweet
Than all of these.

Japanese, 17th century

Baby: an alimentary canal with a loud voice at one end and no responsibility at the other.

ELIZABETH I. ADAMSON

Adam and Eve had many advantages, but the principal one was that they escaped teething.

MARK TWAIN, *Pudd'nhead Wilson*

When the first baby laughed for the first time, the laugh broke into a thousand pieces and they all went skipping about, and that was the beginning of fairies.

JAMES BARRIE, *Peter Pan*

A baby is an angel whose wings decrease as his legs increase.

French proverb

How lovely he appears! his little cheeks
In their pure incarnation, vying with
The rose leaves strewn beneath them.

BYRON, *Cain*

A bit of talcum? Is always walcum.

OGDEN NASH, *Reflection of babies*

Babies are unreasonable; they expect far too much of
existence. Each new generation that comes takes one look
at the world, thinks wildly, 'Is *this* all they've done to it?'
and bursts into tears.

CLARENCE DAY, *The Crow's Nest*

For what she does not know, she eats,
A worm, a twig, a block, a fly,
And every novel thing she meets
Is bitten into by and by.

ROBERT NATHAN, *The Daughter of Evening*

There are times when parenthood seems nothing but
feeding the mouth that bites you.

PETER DE VRIES, *Tunnel of Love*

Man, a dunce uncouth,
Errs in age and youth:
Babies know the truth.

ALGERNON CHARLES SWINBURNE
Cradle Songs

This afternoon at 4.15 at the Imperial Household Hospital,
Her Highness the Crown Princess honorably effecting
delivery, the honorable birth of a son occurred. The
exalted mother and child are honorably healthy.

Japanese Radio announcement of the birth of a Prince.
(*Newsweek*, 7 March 1960)

Born in a Workhouse

ALTHOUGH I AM NOT DISPOSED to maintain that the being born in a workhouse, is in itself the most fortunate and enviable circumstance that can possibly befall a human being, I do mean to say that in this particular instance, it was the best thing for Oliver Twist that could possibly have occurred. The fact is, that there was considerable difficulty in inducing Oliver to take upon himself the office of respiration, – a troublesome practice, but one which custom has rendered necessary to our easy existence; and for some time he lay gasping on a little flock mattress, rather unequally poised between this world and the next: the balance being decidedly in favour of the latter. Now, if, during this brief period, Oliver had been surrounded by careful grandmothers, anxious aunts, experienced nurses, and doctors of profound wisdom, he would most inevitably and indubitably have been killed in no time. There being nobody by, however, but a pauper old woman, who was rendered rather misty by an unwonted allowance of beer; and a parish surgeon who did such matters by contract; Oliver and Nature fought out the point between them. The result was, that, after a few struggles, Oliver breathed, sneezed, and proceeded to advertise to the inmates of the workhouse the fact of a new burden having been imposed upon the parish, by setting up as loud a cry as could reasonably have been expected from a male infant who had been possessed of that very useful appendage, a voice, for much longer space of time than three minutes and a quarter.

CHARLES DICKENS from *Oliver Twist*

Infant Phenomenon

A newborn baby is merely a small, noisy object, slightly fuzzy on one end, with no distinguishing marks to speak of except a mouth, and in colour either a salmon pink or a deep sorrel, depending on whether it is going to grow up a blonde or a brunette. But to its immediate family it is without question the most phenomenal, the most astonishing, the most absolutely unparalleled thing that has yet occurred in the entire history of this planet.

IRVIN S. COBB from *Shakespeare's Seven Ages and Mine*

Nappy Line

I once knew a chap who had a system of just hanging the baby on the clothes line to dry and he was greatly admired by his fellow citizens for having discovered a wonderful innovation on changing a diaper.

DAMON RUNYON from *Diaper Dexterity*

To an Infant Daughter

Sweet gem of infant fairy-flowers!
Thy smiles on life's unclosing hours,
Like sunbeams lost in summer showers,
    They wake my fears;
When reason knows its sweets and sours,
    They'll change to tears.

God help thee, little senseless thing!
Thou, daisy-like of early spring,
Of ambush'd winter's hornet sting
    Hast yet to tell;
Thou know'st not what tomorrows bring:
    I wish thee well.

But thou art come, and soon or late
'Tis thine to meet the frowns of fate,
The harpy grin of envy's hate,
    And mermaid-smiles
Of wordly folly's luring bait,
    That youth beguiles.

And much I wish, whate'er may be
The lot, my child, that falls to thee,

Nature may never let thee see
    Her glass betimes,
But keep thee from my failings free—
    Nor itch at rhymes.

Lord help thee in thy coming years
If thy mad father's picture 'pears
Predominant!—his feeling fears
    And jingling starts;
I'd freely now gi' vent to tears
    To ease my heart.

May thou, unknown to rhyming bother,
Be ignorant as is thy mother,
And in thy manners such another,
    Save sin's nigh quest;
And then with 'scaping this and t'other
    Thou mayst be blest.

Lord knows my heart, it loves thee much;
And may my feelings, aches, and such,
The pains I meet in folly's clutch
    Be never thine:
Child, it's a tender string to touch,
    That sounds 'Thou'rt mine.'

JOHN CLARE

SONNY BOY

WHEN, IN THE SECOND YEAR of his marriage to Rosie M. Banks, the eminent female novelist, his union was blessed and this bouncing boy appeared on the London scene, Bingo's reactions were, I gather, very much the same as yours. Introduced to the child in the nursing home, he recoiled with a startled 'Oi!' and, as the days went by, the feeling that he had run up against something red-hot in no way diminished.

The only thing that prevented a father's love from faltering was the fact that there was in his possession a photograph of himself at the same early age, in which he, too, looked like a homicidal fried egg. This proof that it was possible for a child, in spite of a rocky start, to turn eventually into a suave and polished boulevardier with finely chiselled features heartened him a good deal, causing him to hope for the best.

P. G. WODEHOUSE from *Sonny Boy*

GOLDEN SLUMBERS

Golden slumbers kiss your eyes,
Smiles awake you when you rise.
Sleep, pretty wantons, do not cry,
And I will sing a lullaby;
Rock them, rock them, lullaby.

Care is heavy, therefore sleep you;
You are care, and care must keep you.
Sleep, pretty wantons, do not cry,
And I will sing a lullaby:
Rock them, rock them, lullaby.

THOMAS DEKKER

Born Yesterday

for Sally Amis

Tightly-folded bud,
I have wished you something
None of the others would:
Not the usual stuff
About being beautiful,
Or running off a spring
Of innocence and love –
They will all wish you that,
And should it prove possible,
Well, you're a lucky girl.

But if it shouldn't, then
May you be ordinary;
Have, like other woman,
An average of talents:
Not ugly, not good-looking,
Nothing uncustomary
To pull you off your balance,
That, unworkable itself,
Stops all the rest from working.
In fact, may you be dull –
If that is what a skilled,
Vigilant, flexible,
Unemphasized, enthralled
Catching of happiness is called.

PHILIP LARKIN

LOOKING BACK

WHEN ONE BECOMES A FATHER, then first one becomes a son. Standing by the crib of one's own baby, with that world-old pang of compassion and protectiveness toward this so little creature that has all its course to run, the heart flies back in yearning and gratitude to those who felt just so towards one's self. Then for the first time one understands the homely succession of sacrifices and pains by which life is transmitted and fostered down the stumbling generations of men.

CHRISTOPHER MORLEY from *Mince Pie*

KING OF THE CRADLE

He smiles and clasps his tiny hand,
With sunbeams o'er him gleaming,—
A world of baby fairyland
He visits while he's dreaming.

JOSEPH ASHBY-STERRY from *King of the Cradle*

Parents are the last people on earth who ought to have children.

SAMUEL BUTLER

For our part we have never understood the fear of some parents about babies getting mixed up in hospital. What difference does it make so long as you get a good one?

HEYWOOD BROUN, Pieces of Hate

Babies are necessary to grown-ups. A new baby is like the beginning of all things – wonder, hope, a dream of possibilities. In a world that is cutting down its trees to build highways, losing its earth to concrete, babies are almost the only remaining link with nature, with the natural world of living things from which we spring.

EDA J. LESHAN

Ye are better than all the ballads
    That ever were sung or said;
For ye are living poems,
    And all the rest are dead.

HENRY WADSWORTH LONGFELLOW, Children

A baby is the only person in the house who can leave a ringing telephone alone.

EVAN ESAR

Children need love, especially when they do not deserve it.

HAROLD S. HULBERT

There's a time when you have to explain to your children why and it's a marvellous thing if you know the reason by then.

HAZEL SCOTT

Raising kids is part joy and part guerilla warfare.

EDWARD ASNER

In America there are two classes of travel–first class, and with children. Travelling with children corresponds roughly to travelling third-class in Bulgaria. They tell me there is nothing lower in the world than third-class Bulgarian travel.

ROBERT BENCHLEY, *Kiddie-Kar Travel*

No matter who it is that speaks, or what superlatives are employed, no baby is admired sufficiently to please the mother.

E. V. LUCAS

My father always said that there are four things a child needs–plenty of love–nourishing food–regular sleep–and lots of soap and water–and after those, what he needs most is some intelligent neglect.

IVY BAKER PRIEST

Birth of Winston Churchill

Lord Randolph to Mrs Leonard Jerome

MONDAY 30 (NOVEMBER 1874)
12.30 P.M.

BLENHEIM PALACE
WOODSTOCK

Dear Mrs Jerome,

I have just time to write a line, to send by the London Dr to tell you that all has up to now thank God gone off very well with my darling Jennie. She had a fall on Tuesday walking with the shooters, & a rather imprudent & rough drive in a pony carriage brought on the pains on Saturday night. We tried to stop them, but it was no use. They went on all Sunday. Of course the Oxford physician cld not come. We telegraphed for the London man Dr Hope but he did not arrive till this morning. The country Dr is however a clever man, & the baby was safely born at 1.30 this morning after about 8 hrs labour. She suffered a good deal poor darling, but was vy plucky & had no chloroform. The boy is wonderfully pretty so everybody says dark eyes and hair & vy. healthy considering its prematureness. My mother & Clementine have been everything to Jennie, & she cld not be more comfortable. We have just got a most excellent nurse & wet nurse coming down this afternoon, & please God all will go vy well with both. I telegraphed to Mr Jerome; I thought he wld like to hear. I am sure you will be delighted at this good news and dear Clara also I will write again tonight. Love to Clara.

Yrs affty
RANDOLPH S.C.

I hope the baby things will come with all speed. We have to borrow some from the Woodstock Solicitor's wife.

from *Winston S. Churchill* by RANDOLPH S. CHURCHILL

ON THE BIRTH OF HIS SON

Families, when a child is born
Want it to be intelligent.
I, through intelligence,
Having wrecked my whole life,
Only hope the baby will prove
Ignorant and stupid.
Then he will crown a tranquil life
By becoming a Cabinet Minister.

SU TUNG-P'O (translated from the
11th-century Chinese by Arthur Waley)

THE BATH

THE FIRST BATH which is given to a new-born infant, is usually aided by covering the child from head to foot with cold cream, an operation it is rarely, if ever, necessary to repeat.

Most young mothers take great pride and pleasure in bathing and dressing their little ones, as soon as they are strong enough for the task. Those who do not, either from indisposition or disinclination, lose many a happy hour, full of baby pranks and playful grace.

Yet it seems a dreadful undertaking to a novice, who, as yet, can scarcely hold the soft, delicate little creature, in repose, to think of moving those limp arms and limbs, and turning over and over the plastic body, on which your lightest touch seems to leave an impression, while the heavy head drops and nods, at the risk of falling off, with every movement.

A good stock of courage, patience and strength, should be brought to the first lesson, though, as an established rule, all young mothers *do* cry over it, and are ready to give up twenty times in the undertaking. What matron cannot recall a similar experience, though skill is gained by going through only part of the process at once, under the direction of a competent nurse, who is ready to finish the task when strength gives out. It is better to do this than to wait until you are forced to undertake it, from necessity, and there is no one to appeal to.

from *The Nursery Basket*
Practical Directions for Young Mothers, 1854

The Mother's Song

It is so still in the house.
There is a calm in the house;
The snow storm wails out there,
And the dogs are rolled up with snouts under the tail.

My little boy is sleeping on the ledge,
On his back he lies, breathing through his open mouth
His little stomach is bulging round –
Is it strange if I start to cry with joy?

ESKIMO

Bonie Wee Dochter

Welcome! My bonie, sweet, wee Dochter!
Tho' ye come here a wee unsought for;
And tho' your comin I hae fought for,
    Baith Kirk and Queir;
Yet by my faith, ye 're no unwrought for,
    That I shall swear! . . .

(Lord grant that thou may ay inherit
Thy Mither's looks an' gracefu' merit;
An' thy poor, worthless Daddie's spirit,
    Without his failins!
'Twad please me mair to see thee heir it
    Than stocked mailins!)

For if thou be, what I wad hae thee,
And tak the counsel I shall gie thee,
I'll never rue my trouble wi' thee,
    The cost nor shame o't,
But be a loving Father to thee,
    And brag the name o't. —

ROBERT BURNS from *A Poet's Welcome*
To His Love-Begotten Daughter – the first instance that entitled
him to the venerable appellation of father

Copy

His mother's eyes,
His father's chin,
His auntie's nose,
His uncle's grin,

His great-aunt's hair,
His grandma's ears,
His grandpa's mouth,
So it appears . . .

Poor little tot,
Well may he moan.
He hasn't much
To call his own.

RICHARD ARMOUR

Second Chance

HERE SHE WAS THEN, my daughter, here, alive, the one I must possess and guard. A year before this space had been empty, not even a hope of her was in it. Now she was here, brand new, with our name upon her, and no one could call in the night to reclaim her.

She was here for good, her life stretching before us, and so new I couldn't leave her alone. She was a time-killing lump, her face a sheaf of masks which she'd shuffle through aimlessly. One by one she'd reveal them, while I watched eerie rehearsals of those emotions she would one day need; random, out-of-sequence, but already exact, automatic but strangely knowing – a quick pucker of fury, a puff of ho-hum boredom, a beaming after-dinner smile, perplexity, slyness, a sudden wrinkling of grief, pop-eyed interest, and fat-lipped love.

I'd been handed twenty-odd years wrapped up in this bundle, and hoped to see her grow, learn to totter, to run into the garden, run back, and call this place home. But I realized from these beginnings that I'd got a daughter whose life was already separate from mine, whose will already followed its own directions, and who was quickly correcting my woolly preconceptions of her by being something quite different. She was a child of herself and would be what she was, I was merely the keeper of her temporary helplessness.

But for the rest, I hoped she might be my own salvation, for any man's child is his second chance. In this role I saw her leading me back to my beginnings, re-opening rooms I'd locked and forgotten, stirring the dust in my mind by asking the big questions – as any child could do.

But in my case, perhaps, just not too late; she was already persuading me that there might yet be time, that with her, my tardy but bright-eyed pathfinder, I might return to that wood which long ago I fled from, but which together we might enter and know.

LAURIE LEE from *Two Women*

CRADLE HYMN

See the lovely Babe a-dressing,
Lovely Infant how he smil'd!
When he wept, the Mother's blessing
Sooth'd and hush'd the holy Child.

ISAAC WATTS from *A Cradle Hymn*

Parenthood remains the greatest single preserve of the amateur.

ALVIN TOFFLER

My God, the human baby! A few weeks after birth any other arrival can fend for itself. But you, a basket case until you're twenty-one.

MEGAN TERRY

Babies are bits of star-dust blown from the hand of God. Lucky the woman who knows the pangs of birth for she has held a star.

LARRY BARRETTO, *The Indiscreet Years*

My mother loved children – she would have given anything if I had been one.

GROUCHO MARX

People who say they sleep like a baby usually don't have one.

LEO J. BURKE

A child enters your home and makes so much noise for twenty years you can hardly stand it – then departs, leaving the house so silent you think you will go mad.

DR J.A. HOLMES, *Dynamic Maturity*

Every baby born into the world is a finer one than the last.

CHARLES DICKENS, *Nicholas Nickleby*

It is said that when the Home Secretary of the day congratulated Queen Victoria on the birth of 'a very fine boy' she corrected him to 'a very fine Prince'.

Quoted by ELIZABETH LONGFORD in *Elizabeth R*

One can love a child, perhaps more deeply than one can love another adult, but it is rash to assume that the child feels any love in return.

GEORGE ORWELL, *Collected Essays*

I have given suck, and know
How tender 'tis to love the babe that milks me.

LADY MACBETH

Eat no green apples or you'll droop,
Be careful not get the croup,
Avoid the chicken pox and such,
And don't fall out of windows much.

EDWARD ANTHONY, *Advice to small children*

A baby is an inestimable blessing and bother.

MARK TWAIN

A Good Weight

HE CAME SUDDENLY UPON the master thing in life – birth. He passed through hours of listening, hours of impotent fear in the night and in the dawn, and then there was put into his arms something most wonderful, a weak and wailing creature, incredibly, heart-stirringly soft and pitiful, with minute appealing hands that it wrung his heart to see. He held it in his arms and touched its tender cheek as if he feared his lips might injure it. And this marvel was his Son!

And there was Ann, with a greater strangeness and a greater familiarity in her quality than he had ever found before. There were little beads of perspiration on her temples and her lips, and her face was flushed, not pale, as he had feared to see it. She had the look of one who emerges from some strenuous and invigorating act. He bent down and kissed her, and he had no words to say. She wasn't to speak much yet, but she stroked his arm with her hand and had to tell him one thing.

'He's over nine pounds, Artie,' she whispered.

H.G. WELLS from *Kipps*

THE NEW ARRIVAL

There came to port last Sunday night
*   The queerest little craft,*
Without an inch of rigging on;
*   I looked and looked – and laughed.*
It seemed so curious that she
*   Should cross the unknown water,*
And moor herself within my room –
*   My daughter! O my daughter!*

GEORGE W. CABLE

CUTTING TEETH

IT WAS A PECULIARITY of this baby to be always cutting teeth. Whether they never came, or whether they came and went away again, is not in evidence; but it had certainly cut enough, on the showing of Mrs Tetterby, to make a handsome dental provision for the sign of the Bull and Mouth. All sorts of objects were impressed for the rubbing of its gums, notwithstanding that it always carried, dangling at its waist (which was immediately under its chin), a bone ring, large enough to have represented the rosary of a young nun. Knife-handles, umbrella-tops, the heads of walking-sticks selected from the stock, the fingers of the family in general, but especially of Johnny, nutmeg-graters, crusts, the handles of doors, and the cool knobs on the tops of pokers, were among the commonest instruments indiscriminately applied for this baby's relief. The amount of electricity that must have been rubbed out of it in a week, is not to be calculated. Still Mrs Tetterby always said 'it was coming through, and then the child would be herself'; and still it never did come through, and the child continued to be somebody else.

CHARLES DICKENS from *The Haunted Man*

THE CHILD ASLEEP

(from the French)

Sweet babe! true portrait of thy father's face,
    Sleep on the bosom that thy lips have pressed!
Sleep, little one; and closely, gently place
    Thy drowsy eyelid on thy mother's breast.

Upon that tender eye, my little friend,
    Soft sleep shall come, that cometh not to me!
I watch to see thee, nourish thee, defend;
    'Tis sweet to watch for thee, alone for thee!

His arms fall down; sleep sits upon his brow;
    His eye is closed; he sleeps, nor dreams of harm.
Wore not his cheek the apple's ruddy glow,
    Would you not say he slept on Death's cold arm?

Awake, my boy! – I tremble with affright!
    Awake, and chase this fatal thought! – Unclose
Thine eye but for one moment on the light!
    Even at the price of thine, give me repose!

Sweet error! – he but slept – I breathe again;
    Come, gentle dreams, the hour of sleep beguile!
O, when shall he, for whom I sigh in vain,
    Beside me watch to see thy waking smile?

HENRY WADSWORTH LONGFELLOW

THE BIG SWIM

AFTER A LOT OF REWARDING and enriching pushing, the baby was born . . . As I stood there, with scientific and objective tears rolling down my cheeks, my only thought was 'good gracious it must have taken them years to get these fingernails done so perfectly.' Despite all my training and knowledge, Gremlinology took over instantly. My mind filled with visions of thousands of tiny intra-uterine Japanese engineers building my daughter ('twelve functions as a chronograph, ten functions as a stopwatch and two functions as an alimentary canal'). Her ears were flattened against her temples and I sort of expected to see a little sign saying: 'Loosen transit screws before use to allow ears free movement'. And as we sat there in the delivery room, amid the bloody effluvia and the disposables, the sun streamed in and our daughter started chuckling. I'm telling you it was better than sex or, as they say nowadays, better than hang-gliding . . . From now on, I won't be able to see shots of babies as in *The Ten Commandments* or *Gone With The Wind* without getting lumpy around the throat. I'll be worried about traffic and about men in raincoats. In other words, I'm in the Big Swim; and about time, too.

DR ROB BUCKMAN   from *Out of Practice*

A Child's View

I think babies are lovely. I like them because they are always playful. Sometimes babies break your best china vase or your precious flower pot and you get very cross with them. But you can not blame them because they are very young. All babies get all the praise of the family. And anybody that sees them sometimes say 'isn't she like her mother' or 'oh isn't he a lovely child.' When babies are about ten months old they start to say Ma and Ba. In the park you see lots of babies. Some are laughing some crying. At night babies start to cry, they cry because they want something or they are sad.

ANNE, aged 7

NATIVITY

And she brought forth her first-born son, and wrapped him in swaddling clothes, and laid him in a manger; because there was no room for them in the inn.

And there were in the same country shepherds abiding in the field, keeping watch over their flock by night.

And, lo, the angel of the Lord came upon them, and the glory of the Lord shone round about them: and they were sore afraid.

And the angel said unto them, Fear not: for, behold, I bring you good tidings of great joy, which shall be to all people.

For unto you is born this day in the city of David a Saviour, which is Christ the Lord . . .

But Mary kept all these things, and pondered *them* in her heart.

from *The Gospel According to St. Luke*

To C.F.H.

On Her Christening-Day

*Fair Caroline, I wonder what
You think of earth as a dwelling-spot,
And if you'd rather have come, or not?*

*Today has laid on you a name
That, though unasked for, you will claim
Lifelong, for love or praise or blame.*

*May chance and change impose on you
No heavier burthen than this new
Care-chosen one your future through!*

*Dear stranger here, the prayer is mine
That your experience may combine
Good things with glad . . . Yes, Caroline!*

THOMAS HARDY

There's only one pretty child in the world, and every mother has it.

CHESHIRE PROVERB

Parents are the bones on which children cut their teeth.

PETER USTINOV

A woman who is very anxious to get children always reads storks instead of stocks.

SIGMUND FREUD, Psychopathology of Everyday Life

A child's spirit is like a child, you can never catch it by running after it; You must stand still, and, for love, it will soon itself come back.

ARTHUR MILLER, The Crucible

Children begin by loving their parents. After a time they judge them. Rarely, if ever, do they forgive them.

OSCAR WILDE, A Woman of No Importance

The world has no such flowers in any land,
And no such pearl in any gulf the sea,
As any babe on any mother's knee.

ALGERNON CHARLES SWINBURNE, Pelagius

Nothing grows in our garden, only washing. And babies.

DYLAN THOMAS, *Under Milk Wood*

Parenthood is not what you ought to do: it's what you can stand.

KATHERINE WHITEHORN, *How to Survive Children*

We all of us wanted babies – but did any of us want children?

EDA J. LESHAN

There are only two lasting bequests we can hope to give our children. One of these is roots, the other wings.

HODDING CARTER

The illusions of childhood are necessary experiences: a child should not be denied a balloon because an adult knows that sooner or later it will burst.

MARCELENE COX

A babe is fed with milk and praise.

CHARLES AND MARY LAMB, *The First Tooth*

Intimations of Immortality

Our birth is but a sleep and a forgetting:
The Soul that rises with us, our life's Star,
    Hath had elsewhere its setting,
        And cometh from afar:
        Not in entire forgetfulness,
    And not in utter nakedness,
But trailing clouds of glory do we come
    From God, who is our home . . .

WILLIAM WORDSWORTH
from *Ode: Intimations of*
Immortality from Recollections of Early Childhood

THE COMING OF SIEGFRIED
6 June 1869

A son has arrived!' . . . Now R [Richard Wagner] went back into the salon: from the unconscious mother he heard little more, yet on the other hand he could clearly distinguish the lusty yells of the baby boy. With feelings of sublime emotion he stared in front of him, was then surprised by an incredibly beautiful, fiery glow which started to blaze with a richness of colour never before seen, first on the orange wallpaper beside the bedroom door; it was then reflected in the blue jewel box containing my portrait, so that this, covered by glass and set in a narrow gold frame, was transfigured in celestial spendour. The sun had just risen above the Rigi and was putting forth its first rays, proclaiming a glorious sun-drenched day. R dissolved into tears. Then to me, too, came from across the lake the sound of the early-morning Sunday bells ringing in Lucerne. He looked at the clock and noticed that his son had been born at 4 o'clock in the morning. – Just before 6 o'clock R was allowed in to see me; he told me of his solemn emotions. I was in a mood of cheerfulness and gladness: the gift which Fate had vouchsafed us through the birth of a son appeared to me to be one of immeasurably consoling value. R's son is the heir and future representative of the father for all his children; he will be the protector and guardian of his sisters. We were very happy. The boy is big and strong: they say he weighs two pounds more than other newborn boys. We discussed his name: Siegfried Richard. R felt an urge to give evidence of his joy throughout the house: he had handsome gifts distributed to all the servants.

COSIMA WAGNER from her *Diary*

GOOD WISHES

My dearest Frank, I wish you joy
Of Mary's safety with a boy,
Whose birth has given little pain
Compared with that of Mary Jane.
May he on growing blessing prove
And well deserve his Parents' love!
Endow'd with Art's and Nature's Good,
Thy name possessing with thy Blood,
In him, in all his ways, may we
Another Francis William see!
Thy infant days may he inherit
Thy warmth, nay insolence of spirit
We would not with one fault dispense
To weaken the resemblance . . .
So may his equal faults as Child,
Produce Maturity as mild!
His Saucy words and fiery ways
In early Childhood's pettish days.
In Manhood, shew his Father's mind
Like him, considerate and kind;
All gentleness to those around
And eager only not to wound.

JANE AUSTEN
A poem written to her brother Frank
on the birth of his son

The Baby Smiled

The baby lay in Liffey's arms, snuffling and rooting for food. She sensed its triumph. None of that was important, the baby reproved her; they were peripheral events, leading towards the main end of your life, which was to produce me. You were always the bit part player: that you played the lead was your delusion, your folly. Only by giving away your life, do you save it.

'The little darling,' said Mabs. 'How could anyone hurt a baby?'

The baby smiled.

'Only wind,' said Mabs, startled.

'It was a smile,' said Liffey.

'Babies don't smile for six weeks,' said Mabs, uneasily.

The baby smiled again.

FAY WELDON from *Puffball*

EARLY MORNING FEED

The father darts out on the stairs
To listen to that keening
In the upper room, for a change of note
That signifies distress, to scotch disaster,
The kettle humming in the room behind.

He thinks, on tiptoe, ears-a-strain,
The cool dawn rising like the moon:
'Must not appear and pick him up;
He mustn't think he has me springing
To his beck and call,'
The kettle rattling behind the door.

He has him springing
A-quiver on the landing –
For a distress-note, a change of key,
To gallop up the stairs to him
To take him up, light as a violin,
And stroke his back until he smiles.
He sidles in the kitchen
And pours his tea . . .

And again stands hearkening
For milk cracking the lungs.
There's a little panting,
A cough: the thumb's in: he'll sleep,
The cup of tea cooling on the kitchen table.

Can he go in now to his chair and think
Of the miracle of breath, pick up a book,
Ready at all times to take it at a run
And intervene between him and disaster,
Sipping his cold tea as the sun comes up?

He returns to bed
And feels like something, with the door ajar,
Crouched in the bracken, alert, with big eyes
For the hunter, death, disaster.

PETER REDGROVE

GRANNY WARNING

YOUR MOTHER, or your husband's Mother, may be with you, and you will do well to shew her all possible respect. But let her on no account have the least share in the management of your children. She would undo all that you have done; she would give them their own will in all things. She would humor them to the destruction of their souls, if not their bodies too. Keep the reins in your own hands.

JOHN WESLEY

Spring Moon

S PRING MOON STARED AFTER HER, not wanting to look at the small creature that lay by her side. Tears welled. Reluctantly, she turned toward him. She did not want to know him. She had no right to claim him. The pulsating soft membrane at the crown of the head was vulnerable as a papered window in a storm.

Twice now the chair outside her door had stood empty throughout the length of her labours, empty when the door opened at long last and the announcement was made. And when the preparations were completed no one entered and placed a gold hairpin of gratitude upon her pillow, attesting her husband's esteem and her own fulfilment. No one took her baby . . .to parade with pomp through each court of the homestead, and finally to stand under the lamp of continuous life in the Hall of Ancestors. There was no one to light the incense, guiding the tiny hand with his large one, and announce the glad tidings to all forebears before returning the child to the mother's keeping for the three days of quietness.

Her hand moved to touch the baby's cheek, and the black down on his head. Suddenly she felt a rush of concern so strong that she tore open the quilted cloth and undressed her son, to see if he was really fit, not lame or lacking.

He awoke, kicking furiously, crying to be acknowledged.

This son of ours is beautiful, Spring Moon thought, and has the strength of ten tigers.

BETTE BAO LORD
from Spring Moon – A Novel of China

FRAGMENT

What did my fingers do before they held him?
What did my heart do, with its love?
I have never seen a thing so clear.
His lids are like the lilac-flower
And soft as a moth, his breath.
I shall not let go.

SYLVIA PLATH
from *Three Women*
– A Poem for Three Voices

It is useless to go to bed to save the light, if the result is twins.

Chinese proverb

We are intellectually still babies; this is perhaps why a baby's facial expression so strangely suggests the professional philosopher.

BERNARD SHAW

Families with babies and families without babies are sorry for each other.

E.W. HOWE

Very often birth helps a man to express and enjoy emotions that society primes him to repress.

Dr Miriam Stoppard's Pregnancy and Birth Book

Women say . . .that if men had to have babies there soon would be no babies in the world . . .I have sometimes wished that some clever man would actually have a baby in a new, labour-saving way; then all men could take it up, and one of the oldest taunts in the world would be stilled forever.

ROBERTSON DAVIES, *The Table Talk of Samuel Marchbanks*

Oh, for an hour of Herod!

ANTHONY HOPE (upon emerging from a performance of *Peter Pan*)

If children grew up according to early indications, we should have nothing but geniuses.

J.W. GOETHE

The value of marriage is not that adults produce children but that children produce adults.

PETER DE VRIES, *Tunnel of Love*

A father is a banker provided by nature.

French proverb

The commonest fallacy among women is that simply having children makes one a mother – which is as absurd as believing that having a piano makes one a musician.

SYDNEY J. HARRIS

Children aren't happy with nothing to ignore,
And that's what parents were invented for.

OGDEN NASH, *The Parent*

The Source

THE SLEEP THAT FLITS ON BABY'S EYES – does anybody know from where it comes? Yes, there is a rumour that it has its dwelling where, in the fairy village among shadows of the forest dimly lit with glow-worms, there hang two shy buds of enchantment. From there it comes to kiss baby's eyes.

The smile that flickers on baby's lips when he sleeps – does anybody know where it was born? Yes, there is a rumour that a young pale beam of a crescent moon touched the edge of a vanishing autumn cloud, and there the smile was first born in the dream of a dew-washed morning – the smile that flickers on baby's lips when he sleeps.

The sweet, soft freshness that blooms on baby's limbs – does anybody know where it was hidden so long? Yes, when the mother was a young girl it lay pervading her heart in tender and silent mystery of love – the sweet, soft freshness that has bloomed on baby's limbs.

RABINDRANATH TAGORE

A QUESTION OF UPBRINGING

I KNOW NOT HOW SO WHIMSICAL a thought came into my mind, but I asked, 'If, Sir, you were shut up in a castle, and a new-born child with you, what would you do?' JOHNSON. 'Why, Sir, I should not much like my company.' BOSWELL. 'But would you take the trouble of rearing it?' He seemed, as may well be supposed, unwilling to pursue the subject: but upon my persevering in my question, replied, 'Why yes, Sir, I would; but I must have all conveniences. If I had no garden, I would make a shed on the roof, and take it there for fresh air. I should feed it, and wash it much, and with warm water to please it, not with cold water to give it pain.' BOSWELL. 'But, Sir, does not heat relax.' JOHNSON. 'Sir, you are not to imagine the water is to be very hot. I would not *coddle* the child.'

JAMES BOSWELL
from *The Life of Samuel Johnson* (26 October 1769)

TAKES THREE

It takes three to make a birthday. Most mothers and an increasing number of fathers remember the birth of their first child as the most important experience of their lives. But the person for whom this day is truly vital is neither of you two but the third person; the one who is introduced into the world by your labour: the baby.

PENELOPE LEACH
from *Baby and Child*

THE GREATEST DISCOVERY

Peering out of tiny eyes,
the grubby hands that grip the rail
wiped the window clean of frost,
as the morning air laid on the latch.
A whistle wakened someone there,
next door to the nursery just down the hall,
a strange new sound he'd never heard before,
a strange new sound that makes boys explore.

Tread neat so small those little feet
amid the morning his small heart beats,
so much excitement yesterday
that must be rewarded, must be displayed.
Large hands lift him through the air,
excited eyes contained in there,
the eyes of those he loves and knows,
but what's this extra bed just here?

His puzzled head tips to one side,
amazement swims in those bright green eyes,
glancing down upon this thing
that makes strange sounds,
strange sounds that sing.

In those silent happy seconds
that surround the sound of this event,

a parent's smile is made in moments,
they have made for you a friend.
And all you ever learned from them
until you grew much older
did not compare with when they said
this is your brand new brother,
this is your brand new brother.

Words and music by
ELTON JOHN & BERNIE TAUPIN

BABY BROTHER

MY MUMMY HAD A BABY. It came out of her tummy and it was a BIG surprise. It gave my Mummy a shock but she was glad because she can do the school round again. It is a boy baby. He knew he was a boy all the time but we didn't. He could see out of my Mummy's tummy but we couldn't see in so we didn't know. When he stops crying I hold him on my own but I don't let my friends touch him because he is too small. He is smaller than our cat but he is nicer sometimes.

GILLIAN, aged 7½

Dear Babe

Dear Babe, that sleepest cradled by my side,
Whose gentle breathings, heard in this deep calm,
Fill up the interspersèd vacancies
And momentary pauses of the thought!
My babe so beautiful! it thrills my heart
With tender gladness, thus to look at thee,
And think that thou shalt learn far other lore,
And in far other scenes! For I was reared
In the great city, pent 'mid cloisters dim,
And saw nought lovely but the sky and stars.
But thou, my babe! shalt wander like a breeze
By lakes and sandy shores, beneath the crags
Of ancient mountain, and beneath the clouds,
Which image in their bulk both lakes and shores
And mountain crags: so shalt thou see and hear
The lovely shapes and sounds intelligible
Of that eternal language, which thy God
Utters, who from eternity doth teach
Himself in all, and all things in himself.
Great universal Teacher! he shall mould
Thy spirit, and by giving make it ask.

Therefore all seasons shall be sweet to thee,
Whether the summer clothe the general earth
With greenness, or the redbreast sit and sing
Betwixt the tufts of snow on the bare branch
Of mossy apple-tree, while the nigh thatch
Smokes in the sun-thaw; whether the eave-drops fall
Heard only in the trances of the blast,
Or if the secret ministry of frost
Shall hang them up in silent icicles,
Quietly shining to the quiet Moon.

SAMUEL TAYLOR COLERIDGE from Frost at Midnight

INFANT INNOCENCE

The Grizzly Bear is huge and wild;
He has devoured the infant child.
The infant child is not aware
He has been eaten by the bear.

A.E. HOUSEMAN

Much of a Muchness

On 25 July 1945, our daughter Tamara was born at the Woolavington wing of the Middlesex Hospital in London. She is now a creature of grace and charm, with an expression ever youthful and delicate. Then she was entirely bald, a physical feature she retained for an alarming length of time, and her face had about it much of the secrecy and doggedness of a Soviet field marshall. As I looked at her, trying to kindle feelings of paternity which are entirely intellectual with such tiny children, she stared straight back at me with surprisingly steady blue eyes as though awaiting a complete confession.

My confusion at this inquisitorial gaze was checked by the remark of a swarthy gentleman next to me, who was gazing for the first time at his daughter, in the next slot on the hors d'oeuvre tray. His girl had a full head of black hair and carried an expression of irritation on her small features, as though she couldn't get her castanets to click. 'They're all much of a muchness, aren't they?' he said, heaving with fraternity.

PETER USTINOV from *Dear Me*

BIRTH

Slowly the unborn babe distends life's pathway,
   torn by the child's head;
   Now the living child,
   long cherished by the mother beneath her heart,
Fills the gateway of life.

There is room to pass safely through,
   The child slips downward,
   It becomes visible,
   It bursts into the light of day,
The waters of childbirth flow away.

POLYNESIAN

A Baby's Hands

A baby's hands, like rosebuds furled
Whence yet no leaf expands,
Ope if you touch, though close upcurled,
A baby's hands.

Then, fast as warriors grip their brands
When battle's bolt is hurled,
They close, clenched hard like tightening bands.

No rosebuds yet by dawn impearled
Match, even in loveliest lands,
The sweetest flowers in all the world –
A baby's hands.

ALGERNON CHARLES SWINBURNE